Captain John Smith: American Hero

By Juliana Brennan Rodgers

Illustrated by Noah Bucchi

DEDICATION

Dad: Thank you for introducing me to John Smith, his amazing adventures, and his impact on Jamestown.

Mom: Thank you for inspiring my love of writing and always cheering me on.

SPECIAL THANKS

Noah Bucchi: You are a gifted artist with a very bright future! Thank you for bringing John Smith to life in this book.

Wendy Conrow: Thank you editing this story and for inspiring the next generation of writers. My kids were incredibly lucky to have you as their teacher.

John Smith was:

A soldier

A slave

An escape artist

A sailor

A pirate

An explorer

A captain

A leader

A president

An author

A cartographer (map maker)

A visionary

An adventurer

Who was Captain John Smith?

Many people know John Smith as the English Captain who was saved by a young American Indian girl named Pocahontas. But what you may not have known is that he led a life full of adventure. He traveled to faraway lands, fought as a brave soldier, was captured and made a slave, experienced daring escapes, and sailed aboard a pirate ship! And that's only the beginning of John Smith's story. He went on to become one of the most important American heroes. John Smith was able to see America for what it could be – not just a colony ruled by England but a land so vast and full of promise that anyone who was willing to work hard could be successful.

John Smith was *not* a charming gentleman with proper manners. He was quite the opposite. He was stout and strong but not very tall. What he lacked in height he made up for with a big ego and attitude. He spoke his mind even if it meant angering others. John Smith was bold and adventurous, but he had a lot of common sense as well. John always seemed to find trouble, but fortunately he could talk his way out of just about any situation. And he would need to time and time again.

His Younger Years – A Farmer, a Fan, a Dreamer

John Smith was born in the small village of Willoughby in Lincolnshire, England in 1580. His parents were George Smith and Alice Rickards. He had a younger brother and sister. John's childhood was comfortable -- his family was neither rich nor poor. His father was a farmer who owned a small farm and leased another from Lord Willoughby.

Lord Willoughby was an important and wealthy man. He was kind to John's father and allowed John to attend the school his children attended. This was a privilege, for not all children were allowed to attend such a school. Young John did not like school. The other students were the sons of wealthy and important men called Gentlemen. They made John feel inferior and not worthy of attending school with them. They treated John badly since he was not a son of a

Gentleman. This experience left a strong impression on John, and he spent the rest of his life resentful of Gentlemen.

Although John was smart, he had a difficult time paying attention in school. He was a dreamer who longed for adventure. Sitting in class for hours each day was torture for him. His teacher was not very sympathetic. If John misbehaved, he was beaten by the schoolmaster.

John grew up during an exciting time in history. An English explorer named Francis Drake had circumnavigated the globe by ship. (Circumnavigated means he traveled all the way around the world.) Francis Drake returned to England a hero and was more popular than a modern day movie star. As a young boy, John admired Francis Drake. He dreamed of leading an exciting, adventure-filled life like his hero – Francis Drake.

John didn't just admire Drake because he was the first Englishman to sail around the world. Francis Drake represented how far a farmer's son could make it in the world. Francis Drake was not born into an important, wealthy family. He was not a Gentleman. He earned respect through his own determination and hard work. Queen Elizabeth I knighted Francis Drake in 1580 (the year John was born), and he became *Sir* Francis Drake.

Career Choices – No, Nope, No Way

As the first-born son, John was expected to become a farmer like his father. He would inherit his father's land and run the farm like his father did before him. John did **not** want to become a farmer. He longed for a more adventure-filled life.

He tried his hand at different trades and rejected jobs others would have happily accepted. He was given the opportunity to continue his education, which was not available to everyone, but he declined. When he was 15, he worked as a merchant's apprentice. (An apprentice is a helper, learning the trade.) Becoming a merchant would have made John successful and somewhat wealthy, but it was much too boring for him.

John thought being a soldier would be exciting. He hoped he would become a hero of the battlefield. When John was 16, he fought in the Netherlands. He soon realized his heart was not in it. He felt as if he were fighting men whose beliefs and values were very similar to his own.

Training, Studying, and Preparing

John Smith returned to England. He was 19 years old and was confused about what do to next. He longed for adventure and for an opportunity to make a name for himself. Then he met Theodore Paleologue. Theodore was an Italian man and a direct descendant of Constantine XI - the last Greek emperor of the Eastern Roman Empire. Theodore was one of the most famous horsemen in Europe. He taught John how to ride a horse at full speed with complete control and agility. He taught him how to use his weapon skillfully while riding a horse.

Theodore told John incredible stories about the Ottoman Turks and the war called The Crusades happening in Eastern Europe. John learned the Turks were trying to take over Europe and spread their religion throughout the land. John was captivated by the stories of Christians, like himself, defending their land and beliefs from the Turks. Now this was a fight he believed in! John decided to join these men and fight the Turks.

As John prepared himself to fight in The Crusades, he read several books on the art of war. He continued to train with Theodore Paleologue on fighting strategies, horsemanship, and hunting. John trained and worked hard for a year until he was in top condition and ready to help the Christians win The Crusades. Little did he know that these skills would not only help him in The Crusades, but they'd also help prepare him for his time in America.

Joining the Crusades (…finally some adventure!)

John was excited about this adventure. He would travel to Austria where some of the fighting was taking place. John boarded a ship to Northern France for the first leg of his journey. While on board, John met four friendly Gentlemen and enjoyed the voyage in their company. Once they reached the port in northern France, they locked John in his cabin and took all of his belongings. These were not Gentlemen after all - they were thieves! John had nothing left except the clothes on his back. He searched for the thieves in France, hoping to get his possessions back, but had no luck. Having no other choice, John began his journey to southern France on foot.

John relied on the kindness of strangers for food and shelter while traveling this great distance. One day John was resting under a tree, tired from his long journey, when he met a kind man. John and the man began talking and became friends. The man was the Count of Plouer. He felt sorry for John, so he gave him clothes and money for his journey. John Smith was very thankful to the Count of Plouer for his help.

John finally made it to Marseille, France where he boarded a ship bound for Italy. All of the other passengers on the ship were Roman Catholic. Shortly after the ship set sail, there was a huge storm. The passengers were terrified as the ship was tossed on massive waves. They became convinced that God was angry with them for allowing an English Protestant on board. They were talking about John Smith! The passengers threw him overboard. John was stunned and couldn't believe they would do such a thing. As he struggled in the cold water and churning waves, John spotted an island in the distance. He swam to the island and dragged himself on shore, exhausted and cold.

Early the next morning, John woke to find the storm had passed. He began to wonder how he would get off the island. Just then he saw a ship in the distance. He desperately flagged down the ship and was relieved when they saw him and began to get closer. But his relief was short-lived as he realized he had just flagged down a pirate ship! The pirates brought John on board. (He really had no other choice.) John must have wondered, "What am I going to do *now*?" But if there was one thing he was good at, it was talking himself out of sticky situations. While talking to the Pirate Captain, he realized they had a mutual friend - the Count of Plouer! The Pirate Captain decided that John must be a good man to be the Count of Plouer's friend, so he welcomed John onboard and promised to take him to Italy.

Along the way, the pirates plundered several ships. John must have helped because when they dropped him off in Italy, they gave him his share of the booty—500 gold coins!

John Smith becomes *Captain* John Smith

John joined The Crusades in the summer of 1601. At only 21 years old, he was young but quickly made a name for himself. All of his training and preparations with Theodore

14

Paleologue began to pay off. During one battle, John suggested they trick the enemy in order to defeat them. In those days, they used guns called matchlock muskets. These guns had a small fuse which remained lit. This flame glowed and was visible in the darkness. John explained that if they waited until darkness and then lit many tiny matches, the enemy would assume the tiny flames were guns and believe they were facing a much larger army. They lit over 3,000 matches. The enemy panicked and was defeated. John's idea worked perfectly! He was given credit and the title of Captain. John was very proud of his new title. He went by Captain John Smith for the rest of his life.

Jousting Tournament – Three Heads and a Coat of Arms

In the spring of 1602, at the age of 22, John and his troops were preparing to attack a walled city in Hungary. Before the battle began, the Lord of the city issued a challenge to any English officer. Many of the English officers wanted to be the one chosen to accept this challenge, so they drew lots. John won and was selected to accept the challenge. The challenge was a joust... to the death. John had been taught well by Theodore Paleologue during his months of training in England. He knew the weakest part on a suit of armor was the visor. John aimed his lance directly at his opponent's visor and won!

The beaten (and dead) man's friend became enraged and challenged John to another jousting match. John accepted without hesitation. The man's name was Grualgo. On the first pass, they used lances. Their lances slammed into one another and shattered. On the second pass, they used pistols. Grualgo's shot hit John, but fortunately his armor protected him. John shot and hit Grualgo in the arm. Grualgo was unable to control his horse with an injured arm and was thrown to the ground. John dismounted and approached with his sword. John later told friends that Grualgo "lost his head, as his friend before."

John was now feeling proud of himself and unbeatable, so he issued a challenge of his own inviting someone of rank to dual him. A man named Bonny Mulgro accepted. On the first pass, the men used pistols. Neither man was hit. On the second pass, they used battle-axes. Bonny knocked John's axe to the ground. The jousting rules stated that John must make another pass without his battle-axe. The only weapon John had was a short, broad sword called a falchion. John was riding to his death. How could he possibly survive? As they rode toward each other, John did the unimaginable.

Against all odds, as the massive battle-axe was swinging toward him, John held his horse's reins tightly and leaned as far out of the way as possible. The battle-axe missed him by a hair. As they passed, John turned and quickly thrust the blade of his falchion in the exact spot where the two plates of armor met on his opponent's back. John won for the third time!

The leader of the regiment, Prince Zsigmond of Transylvania, was impressed with John's performance. He gave John a generous reward: a coat of arms, a portrait in gold, and money. John designed his coat of arms with three fancy Turkish heads and the motto, "Vincere est Vivere," which means, "To Conquer Is To Live." According to English tradition, a man with a coat of arms had the right to call himself an English Gentleman. Like his hero Sir Francis Drake, John Smith had earned the title of Gentleman not by being born into it, but by his own determination, bravery, and perhaps a touch of luck.

John Smith's Luck Runs Out

John Smith traveled to Transylvania where he continued to fight in The Crusades. A fierce battle took place in which he and his men were seriously outnumbered. John and his troops were badly defeated, and tens of thousands of soldiers were killed. John was injured, captured, and sold into slavery. A man named Bashaw Bogall purchased John as a slave. John was chained to several other slaves and forced to walk 500 miles to Constantinople.

Bashaw liked a beautiful, young woman named Charatza Tragabigzanda. He thought he would impress Charatza by giving her a slave, so he gave John Smith to her as a gift. Both she and John spoke a little Italian, so they were able to communicate. John regaled Charatza with stories of his adventures. She was captivated by this brave Englishman and fell in love with him.

Charatza may have been young, but she was wise enough to know that if her parents found out she was in love with a slave there would be trouble. She feared that John would be sent away forever. She decided to take matters into her own hands. Charatza thought John would be safe if she sent him to work on her brother's farm far out in the country for a few years until she became old enough to make her own decisions. She wrote a note to her brother asking him to take this slave until she called for him again.

Unfortunately, her brother figured out what was going on and was furious with John. He shaved John's head and beard, placed a thick iron ring around his neck, forced him to wear an itchy hair coat, and treated him as the lowest slave. Many horrible months passed for John living as a slave.

Charatza's brother had a fierce temper and often beat the slaves. One day, John was working alone in the wheat fields when the brother approached him on horseback. He began to beat John ruthlessly. John knew he must take action, or he would be killed. He swung his wheat-threshing bat at the brother and knocked him off his horse. John beat him, hid him under a pile of straw, dressed in his clothes, and took his horse. It was a desperate and unlikely escape attempt, but he had no other choice. John could easily be identified as a slave because of his shaved head and the thick iron ring around his neck.

John was afraid he would be caught and forced to return to slavery, or worse, killed. He rode for 16 days straight until he finally reached a Russian military unit. The governor listened to John's story and removed the iron ring from John's neck. John had made it to freedom!

Now that he was safe, John spent the next several months touring Europe. He had a natural curiosity about how people lived in different lands. He didn't judge them for being different, as many Englishmen would have in his day. Instead, he studied them and learned from them. He learned that although people may live differently, it didn't mean that they were any less important. This lesson would greatly impact his relationship with the American Indians and would help him better understand and communicate with them.

Returning to England – Preparing for the Trip of a Lifetime

In 1604, John Smith returned to England. It was a very different England than the one he had left more than three years before. England's beloved Queen Elizabeth I had died. She had been the only Queen John Smith had ever known. Queen Elizabeth had focused her energy on her people and strengthening England. Since she had never married nor had children, her cousin James became the King of England. King

James was not as focused on England; instead, he wanted to conquer and acquire lands around the world.

As John rode through London, England's capital, he noticed the turmoil his homeland was experiencing. London was very crowded with poor people looking for work. Crime was high, and sewage ran down the filthy streets. Worst of all, a deadly disease called the plague was spreading quickly through the country, killing many people.

While in London, John met Bartholomew Gosnold. Bartholomew had been to America and thought it would be wise for England to start a colony there. He saw it as a chance for England to help some of its citizens by giving them a new land to live in. He recognized John's talents and strengths and thought he would be a strong addition to the group. He invited John to join them. John, as always, was eager for adventure and readily agreed to join the travelers.

Planning a journey of over 5,000 miles took time. They had many things to do:

- Convince people to make the difficult and dangerous trip.

- Raise money to buy materials and food needed for the five-month journey.

- Convince King James to approve of the expedition.

John did not like to be idle – he preferred action! Although he was restless, he used this time wisely. He prepared for his American adventure by learning things that would help him while he was in Virginia. He learned some of the native language that would be key in his dealings with the American Indians in Virginia. John also learned how to make maps. This was important since they were traveling to a place few Englishmen had ever been.

After nearly two years of preparations, the time had come. The Virginia Company of London paid for the trip to America. They were a group of investors hoping to make money. They wanted the expedition to accomplish three goals:

#1. <u>Find gold</u>. There were wild stories about gold washing up on the shores of America.

#2. <u>Find the Northwest Passage to the South Sea</u>. The English believed there was a waterway that would take them through America to the Pacific Ocean. This would enable them to travel to the Orient for trade without having to travel over land where they were often attacked or charged more for goods.

#3. <u>Find survivors of the Lost Colony</u>. Several years earlier, a group of English settlers attempted to start a colony in Roanoke, Virginia. They disappeared and were never seen nor heard from again.

The Voyage to Virginia – Rough Seas, Seasickness, and an Enemy

Captain Christopher Newport was named commander of the expedition. He was a tall, one-armed sea captain with over 20 years experience on the seas whose very presence commanded respect. He was known for his courage, and he even fought alongside John's hero, Sir Francis Drake. Captain Newport had made many trips to the West Indies, just south of Virginia, so he knew the waters well. Even the brash, young John couldn't help but admire Captain Newport. Little did John know that he would end up owing his life to the Captain.

On December 20, they set sail on three ships - *The Susan Constant*, *The God Speed*, and *The Discovery*. The ships were not large and had very crowded conditions with people sleeping on top of crates filled with food supplies, casks of water, and tools, and alongside livestock such as chickens, sheep, and goats. Seventy-one people (54 passengers and 17 crew) crossed the Atlantic in the *Susan Constant*. The *God Speed* carried 52 (39 passengers and 13 crew) and the *Discovery* carried 21 (12 passengers and nine crew). In all there were 144 men and boys on the expedition (105 passengers and 39 crew). Of the passengers on board, there were more than 50 Gentlemen, 12 laborers, four carpenters, four boys, two bricklayers, a priest, a sail maker, a mason, a blacksmith, a surgeon, a tailor, and a drummer.

Events got off to a rocky start. Just as they were setting sail to leave England, the winds suddenly changed and began to blow in the wrong direction. In those days, ships did not have motors. They relied on sails and needed to get out into the ocean where the trade winds would carry them. The three ships had to wait until the wind direction changed again. They dropped anchor and waited, bobbing in the stormy waters within sight of England for several weeks! You can imagine the terrible seasickness the landlubbers endured. Finally, the winds changed, and they began their journey.

It took 144 days - 4 ½ long months - at sea before they reached Virginia. Even the most patient person would become restless, and John Smith was not known for his patience. To make matters worse, half of those on board were Gentlemen who irritated John. They thought they were more important than anyone else. Although John had been named an English Gentleman due to his bravery in battle, the other Gentlemen did not believe him to be a *true* Gentleman because he was not born one. He had earned the title, but they did not respect John as a Gentleman. This made John angry and frustrated.

John passed the time by telling stories of his adventures to the boys onboard the ship. Everyone who overheard the tales of his many battles, victories, escapes, and travels must have been impressed. The crew and the boys admired John. The Gentlemen resented this and were jealous. John loved it – he enjoyed antagonizing those irritating Gentlemen.

Before long, John had made a powerful enemy. Edward Wingfield (always known as "Wingfield") represented everything John disliked. He was a Gentleman from a well-known and wealthy family. He had been handed everything without working for it and made it a point to tell everyone just how important he was. Wingfield was jealous of John's friendships with the men onboard. He decided he would get rid of John Smith, so he reported to Captain Newport that John was trying to gather the men and take over the ship. (In seafaring terms, this was known as mutiny.) Wingfield insisted that John be hanged at their next stop in the Canary Islands.

Most men would have been terrified or outraged by such a charge, but not John. He laughed off Wingfield's accusations. Captain Newport did not believe the charges against John and refused to have John hanged. But Captain Newport had a responsibility to make sure the journey was as peaceful as possible. With over 3,200 miles and two months still to travel, Captain Newport thought it would be best if the two men remained apart. He ordered John to remain below deck.

John and Wingfield continued to argue over the next few weeks. When they landed on the island of Nevis in the West Indies to replenish supplies, Wingfield was determined to see John hanged. While Captain Newport was distracted, Wingfield had a gallows quickly built. Again John laughed at Wingfield, which infuriated him. John had several friends stand by him and protect him. Captain Newport returned and again refused to allow Wingfield to hang John. But Captain Newport realized he had to do something. Wingfield was an important man and was accusing John of the serious crime of mutiny. In order to appease Wingfield, Captain Newport ordered John to spend the remainder of the voyage below deck in shackles. They would work it out once they arrived in Virginia. John was safe again... but not exactly comfortable.

Why did Captain Newport save John? Why not side with a Gentleman of importance such as Wingfield? Perhaps Captain Newport knew more than he was letting on. You see, the Virginia Company had sent along a secret box. This box contained a list of the men on the voyage who would be named to the Governing Council and would be in charge of running the colony. The box was *only* to be opened once they reached Virginia.

Arriving in Virginia – Jamestown, the Secret Box, and Sickness

On April 26, 1607, the three ships sailed into the Chesapeake Bay carrying 104 passengers and 39 crew. (One passenger died on the journey.) John Smith, a man who would be so important to the English settlement, arrived as a prisoner in shackles.

The land of Virginia was dramatically different than England. Jamestown was a swamp with brackish water. It was filled with creatures such as turtles, frogs, and snakes. The weather was muggy and much warmer than England. On May 13, they found a suitable location to settle and named it Jamestown in honor of King James of England.

Soon after arriving, they opened the secret box. The list of men named to the Governing Council included six Gentlemen and... John Smith! The Gentlemen, especially Wingfield, were shocked and angry that John would be joining them on the Council. Wingfield decided to take matters into his own hands. Before John was released from his shackles and allowed to join the Council, Wingfield was voted to be the President of the Council at Jamestown.

Throughout the summer, the men searched for gold and the Northwest Passage. After two months, Captain Newport left Jamestown and set sail for England. He would bring news to the Virginia Company. Soon after Captain Newport left, a terrible sickness spread throughout Jamestown. At the beginning of summer, there were 104 men in Jamestown. By the end of summer only 50 men were left - over half had died!

John noticed that while many men were suffering and dying, Wingfield seemed healthy and well fed. He discovered that Wingfield was keeping the most nourishing food for himself and his friends and not giving enough to the rest of the men. While this didn't cause the sickness spreading throughout Jamestown, it certainly didn't help the sick men regain their strength. The men were outraged at Wingfield. The Council removed Wingfield from command and placed John Ratcliffe in charge. Ratcliffe wasn't much better, but at least he recognized John Smith's strengths. He placed John in charge of trading. Ratcliffe wanted John to establish a good relationship with the American Indians and trade for much needed food. John took several men upriver. Little did John Smith know he was about to embark on another historic adventure!

John Smith Meets Chief Powhatan and Pocahontas

While exploring upriver, John left several men in the boat while he, an American Indian guide, and two of his men hiked inland, away from the river. It wasn't long before a group of American Indians ambushed John and his men. Thinking quickly, John realized they would not kill one of their own, so he tied his arm to the guide's arm and used him as a shield. His men were killed, but John fought bravely even though there were over 200 American Indians! They were amazed that this man would fight so fearlessly even when so incredibly outnumbered.

The guide strapped to John Smith's arm feared for his life. He was their only hope of surviving this predicament. The guide explained to the other American Indians that John was a "werowance" ("leader") and that his life must be spared until another werowance decided his fate. They ordered John to lay down his weapons. John remembered several years earlier when he was captured and forced into slavery and he was afraid it would happen again. He wasn't going without a fight, so he refused to give up his weapons. He began to back up but slipped into a frozen swamp. As he sank lower in the cold, quicksand-like mud he realized that he was beaten. He laid down his weapon and the American Indians pulled him out.

They brought John to Opechancauough, the ruler of the region. John knew he had to impress Opechancauough in order to survive. Thinking quickly, John pulled a compass from his pocket. Opechancauough had never seen anything like the compass and was amazed. John breathed a sigh of relief and thought his life was saved, but Opechancauough gave a signal and his men suddenly grabbed John, tied him to a tree, drew their arrows, and pointed them directly at John Smith. There was no way he could escape this time, but John did not show fear. He stood bravely, looking the warriors in the eye, and awaited his fate. Again, they were impressed by this display of courage. They untied John and brought him back to their camp.

They showed John to a longhouse (a type of American Indian house) and gave him food. John was hungry but afraid the food might be poisoned. Once he realized the food was not poisoned, he began to eat. They brought him more and more food. John wondered fearfully if perhaps they were trying to fatten him up so they could eat him! Luckily for John, this was not true. John spent the next few weeks being taken from village to village.

Finally, John was taken to see the chief of all the tribes in the region. Chief Wahunsonacock was the ruler of over 30 tribes of Powhatan Indians. He was known to the English as "Chief Powhatan." Chief Powhatan lived in a place called Werowocomoco ("King's House"). As John Smith arrived at Werowocomoco, he compared it to Jamestown. Jamestown sat in a swampy area near the sea, so the ships could easily load and unload. Werowocomoco was located 12 miles up the York River. It was a beautiful area surrounded by fields of corn, tobacco, beans, and sunflowers.

John was taken into Chief Powhatan's enormous longhouse. It was the size of half a football field. The longhouse was filled with over 200 important American Indian leaders from throughout the region. They were painted red from the shoulders up and all gave a great shout when John entered the room. If John felt intimidated, he didn't show it.

Chief Powhatan spoke to John Smith in Algonquian, the language Powhatan Indians of Virginia spoke. John had wisely studied Algonquian in England while waiting for the voyage to launch. Chief Powhatan asked John many questions. Most importantly, he wanted to know what the English were doing in his land and how long they planned to stay. John decided it would be safest if he lied to Chief Powhatan about this topic. John told him they were chased by a Spanish ship and shipwrecked here. He said Captain Newport would be returning to bring them back to England.

John asked many questions of Chief Powhatan. As ruler of a vast region, Chief Powhatan would have considerable knowledge about his land. John asked Chief Powhatan how far it was to the Pacific Ocean and if there was a river that would take him there by boat. Chief Powhatan did not supply any useful information about the location of such a river because it didn't exist.

Everything seemed to be going well between the two men when suddenly Chief Powhatan gave a signal, and his men grabbed John. They forced him to place his head upon a large boulder and held him down. Warriors approached with large clubs ready to bash John's head. Although he had escaped death many times before, John saw no way out of this. He closed his eyes and prepared to die.

Suddenly, John heard a small voice pleading with Chief Powhatan. It was Chief Powhatan's feisty ten-year-old daughter, Pocahontas. She stepped forward and spoke rapidly to her father asking him to spare John Smith's life. Chief Powhatan refused, but Pocahontas did not give up. She was afraid John would be killed before she could convince her father, so she rushed to John's side and laid her head on top of his to protect him. Her father was surprised and touched by Pocahontas's actions. Pocahontas was Chief Powhatan's favorite daughter. Pocahontas was her nickname and meant, "playful one." Her real name was Mataoka. Chief Powhatan agreed to spare John Smith's life.

Legend (and the Disney movie) transformed this scene into a love story, but the facts show that is not true. Pocahontas was only ten or eleven years old. There was a mutual respect and admiration for each other's bravery, but never a romance. When you think about it, John Smith and Pocahontas had similar characteristics. They were bold, adventurous, brave, and willing to face danger for what they believed in. Although Pocahontas may have had a schoolgirl's crush on the brave Englishman, John thought of her like a daughter.

Modern day historians believe the scene that took place between John Smith and Pocahontas in Chief Powhatan's longhouse may have been an American Indian ceremony. According to the ritual, just as the Chief is about to kill the prisoner, he stops as if to say, "This is what I *could* do to you, but I'm not going to because I would rather have you as a friend." The Chief then welcomes the prisoner into the tribe. We may never know the truth, but this scene has forever become an American legend.

After the ceremony, Chief Powhatan welcomed John into his tribe as if he were a member of the family. He even offered to make John the chief of his own tribe. John thanked him but refused. Chief Powhatan told John that as a new member of the tribe, he should go to Jamestown and return with gifts for his new Powhatan Indian "family." Chief Powhatan specifically requested two cannons and a grindstone. John agreed (in order to be released) and returned to Jamestown with an escort. The English were stunned to see John walk out of the forest with the Powhatan

Captain John Smith: American Hero

Indians. They thought he had been killed weeks ago along with the other men on the expedition.

John had no intention of giving the Powhatan Indians such powerful weapons such as the cannons. He made it a point never to trade weapons for goods. These people could become his enemy very quickly, so he did not want to supply them with weapons.

Over time, the American Indians had acquired a few firearms, usually stolen from a colonist, but they did not understand how to use them. One time, a group got hold of a bag of gunpowder, and the men were killed when they mishandled it. Another time, a group tried to plant gunpowder to see if they could grow more. Their lack of understanding of these weapons kept them from being a threat. Besides, the American Indians had the advantage because they far outnumbered the colonists.

John had tricked Chief Powhatan when he agreed to send the cannons back. John knew each cannon weighed well over one ton, so there would be no way the Powhatan

Indians could carry them back to Werowocomoco. John must have been chuckling to himself as they strained, tugged, and pulled – trying to carry the enormous cannons. John decided to give them a show. He demonstrated the cannon's power for them by loading it with rocks and aiming it at a frozen tree. It made such a loud boom that the Powhatan Indians ran away with fear. John laughed and coaxed them back. The grindstone was also too heavy to carry, so John sent toys and trinkets for Chief Powhatan and his family.

The very same day John returned to Jamestown after weeks of being held captive by the Powhatan Indians, several of his fellow colonists (including his old enemy, Wingfield) set out to get him. They secretly wanted to return to England. They were tired of starving, working hard, and the grueling conditions. They knew John would never agree to return to England and he would prevent them from leaving, so they ruled that John should be put to death because he was responsible for the men who were killed on the expedition.

They raised the gallows the very next morning and walked John up to the noose. Again John faced certain death with no way out. Just as he stepped up and was about to be hanged, a yell from the crowd announced a ship on the horizon. Captain Newport had returned, and John Smith was saved... again.

Searching for the Northwest Passage, Map Making, and a Stingray

In the summer of 1608, John Smith led an expedition of the Chesapeake Bay, exploring its many tributaries. He hoped to accomplish several things:

1) Discover the Northwest Passage which would bring him fame.

2) Establish relations and trade with more American Indians in the region.

3) Make detailed maps of the area.

The expedition proved to be very difficult. Several times, his men were worried they had traveled too far upriver. The land was wild, and they saw many fearsome creatures, such as bear, at the water's edge. John listened to their fears and told them not to be afraid. He promised he would stand by them and protect them if they came across danger. The men knew John was a courageous leader and he spoke the truth. They followed his example of being brave.

During one point in the trip the men were very hungry. They could see a large school of fish in the shallow water, but they didn't have any fishing poles or equipment to fish. John took out his sword and began stabbing it into the water. It worked! The men joined, and in one hour, they had enough fish to feed the crew for the entire day. The men began celebrating their success and their excitement for the upcoming feast when things suddenly turned tragic. As John was taking the fish off his sword, he felt a sharp pain in his upper arm. One of the fish he had caught was a deadly stingray. It lashed its sharp tail and struck John. Its poisonous venom was spreading quickly through John's arm. His hand, arm, and shoulder became red and swollen. John thought this deadly venom would kill him, so he ordered his men to dig his grave. John was still in charge, even when he thought he was dying! Luckily, the doctor used medicinal oil, and it began to heal John's arm. John had escaped death yet again… and he ATE the stingray for dinner!

John Smith accomplished many things during the Chesapeake Bay expedition that summer. He created a map covering the 200-mile long Chesapeake Bay and many of its tributaries. He was an excellent mapmaker, and his detail was so accurate that the map was used for over 300 years. He also met many American Indian tribes, and by displaying his strength but also his kindness, he won the respect of nearly all of them. However, John was disappointed when the summer came to an end, and he had not found the Northwest Passage. He could not have known there was none to be found. The Pacific Ocean was 3,000 miles away, and no waterway would lead him there.

John did not look forward to returning to Jamestown. It seemed every time he returned, things were in chaos or the settlers wanted to hang him. Fortunately, the 12 men John had just spent the summer with believed in him, admired his abilities, and trusted him. They learned he was a good leader. When they returned, John Smith was elected President of Jamestown.

John Smith Becomes President of Jamestown

During this time in history, England was segregated into different "classes." The men from important families were considered upper class and were often Gentlemen. The lower classes were called "commoners." The commoners did physical work such as building shelter and gathering food. Gentlemen did not do hard physical labor. The Gentlemen did not work at Jamestown, which meant about 30 men (commoners) worked to support and feed 200 men. Does this seem fair to you? John Smith didn't think this was fair either.

During the summer months, the Jamestown settlers lived in makeshift tents. With winter quickly approaching, John knew they would need to build shelters in order to protect themselves against the cold weather. In order to construct shelter, John decided they would need *everyone's* help. As the President of Jamestown, he made a rule. He said: "He that will not work shall not eat." It was simple, but many of the Gentlemen were outraged. John had no trouble standing up to these men. He knew in this tough land, they would all need to work in order to survive. The Gentlemen were not happy but grudgingly began to work. Soon Jamestown started to look like a settlement instead of just a temporary campground.

The men respected President Smith because he worked alongside them, often doing the hardest tasks himself. Things were finally beginning to go well. John had been in charge for less than one month, and already they were seeing progress. They built 20 new houses inside the fort, dug a well so they would have clean drinking water, and cleared 40 acres of land for planting.

John also taught the men how to conduct themselves like the troops he worked with during The Crusades. He would take the men out to do drills, such as marching in orderly lines and shooting at trees for target practice. He would have the men do these things within plain view of the American Indians so they could see how well-trained and fearsome the Englishmen and their guns were. This was all part of John's plan to earn their fear and respect. With thousands of American Indians in the area and only a few dozen settlers,

John knew the American Indians could easily overpower the English. The one advantage the English settlers had was their guns, so John demonstrated gun power often.

Under President Smith, Jamestown was finally functioning well, but things were about to change yet again. Captain Newport returned bringing 80 men and two women. John was furious to learn that the Virginia Company had again sent mostly Gentlemen, not hard-working men that the difficult conditions in Virginia required. He was not angry, however, that they had sent women. He knew women were important to establishing a permanent settlement. He saw this as a good sign.

Almost immediately after his arrival, Captain Newport took 100 of the strongest men on an expedition to search for the Northwest Passage. He left John with the weakest men, but John was determined. Again, he required every person to work and contribute. It was the only way they would survive. The newly arrived Gentlemen resisted working, but when

John worked hard alongside them, they began to appreciate the hard work and felt proud to be contributing.

The Gentlemen who had just arrived had "soft hands" since they were not used to physical work such as cutting down trees. Soon many of them had blisters on their hands. Work became painful for these men, so many would curse with each blow of their axe. It may seem funny that a tough soldier like John Smith would dislike foul language, but he was determined that his men would not swear. Throughout the day John would keep track of those who swore. Then at dinnertime he would pour one cup of water down their sleeve for each swear word they had said that day. It was definitely an unusual method, but it worked. Soon not a swear word was heard among the men.

During his time as President of Jamestown, John established enough trading with the local American Indians to keep the colonists well fed. He would trade trinkets, toys, tools, or copper for food.

The Powhatan Indians Want the English to Leave

Chief Powhatan learned that John Smith had lied to him when he told Chief Powhatan the English were not in Virginia to stay. He feared for his people, his land, his culture, and his way of life. Chief Powhatan knew his people would be in great danger if the English decided to stay in Virginia permanently.

The relationship between the Powhatan Indians and the English settlers began to break down. Many years before the English arrived at Jamestown, a Powhatan Indian priest told Chief Powhatan that a tribe would rise from the Chesapeake Bay and destroy his empire. Chief Powhatan began to believe the English in Jamestown would make this prediction come true, so he ordered his people to stop trading food with the English.

Once Chief Powhatan realized the English were planning to stay, he decided he needed to drive them out of his land before there were too many to overcome. This was very insightful of Chief Powhatan. When the English landed at

Jamestown in 1607, there were over 14,000 Powhatan Indians in the area. The Powhatan Indians easily outnumbered the 104 colonists. Just 50 years later, the Powhatan Indian population had dwindled to only 1,000. In contrast, the English population in 1657 was up to a staggering 25,000.

The relationship between the English settlers and the Powhatan Indians also became strained during this time because Virginia was experiencing a drought. At times of drought, when water was scarce, the Powhatan Indians' crops were affected. They kept extra food for times of drought and other emergencies. If they had a good season and did not need the extra food, they would use it to trade with the English for goods and tools. However, as the drought went on for season after season, they needed their food reserves to feed their own people. Since the English depended upon the Powhatan Indians for food, they became angry and frustrated when the Powhatan Indians no longer traded or provided food. The Powhatan Indian-English relationship became tense.

Chief Powhatan was a smart man. He realized that John Smith was the reason Jamestown was successful and growing. He plotted to have John killed during an attack on Jamestown. Pocahontas warned John of the attack and saved his life once again.

John Smith Suffers a Serious Injury

In September 1609, John Smith's lifetime of luck ran out. He was returning from checking on some of the settlers upriver, when he fell asleep lying in the bottom of the boat. A spark from a flintlock gun landed on his gunpowder pouch, which was strapped to his waist, and caught fire. Thinking quickly, John tumbled over the side of the boat into the water. The fire was instantly extinguished, but John was seriously injured and nearly drowned. His men pulled him into the boat. He was badly burned from his waist to his thighs and was in terrible pain. There was no doctor on the boat, so John had to endure the pain for the 100-mile trip back to Jamestown.

When he finally arrived at Jamestown, his condition had gotten worse. John's rivals took advantage of his weakness and forced him to give up the Presidency. John was in too much pain to put up a fight. A ship heading back to England was leaving Jamestown the next day. John was in need of medical care that he could receive only in England, so he asked the captain if he could be a passenger.

On October 4, 1609, John Smith left Virginia. He would spend the rest of his life trying to return to the land he had grown to love.

Jamestown Without John Smith – The Starving Time

Things fell apart quickly at Jamestown after John Smith left. The winter of 1609-1610 was devastating and is referred to as "The Starving Time." The English had eaten all the food they had and the since Powhatan Indians would not provide any additional food, they soon ran out. They were not able to leave the fort to hunt or search for anything such as snakes, frogs, or roots because the Powhatan Indians would attack anyone outside the fort. The men became desperate. They ate the horses and livestock, then the cats and dogs, and then rats and mice. When those were gone, they ate any leather items such as boots and shoes. Many people starved to death.

The English started the winter with over 500 people, but by spring only 60 men were left. It must have been a horrible winter for the colonists to endure. On May 21, 1610, a ship arrived at Jamestown. The crew aboard was shocked to find the Jamestown survivors crying, "We are starved!"

The ship carried a supply of food that would last only one week. The men on the ship were frightened by the devastation they saw and decided to abandon Virginia. On June 7, the starving settlers gave shouts of joy as they boarded the ship bound for England. They were happy to leave the land that had defeated them. Just as the ship was sailing down toward the Chesapeake, an amazing twist of fate occurred. Another ship carrying 300 healthy colonists and a full year's supply of food arrived. Jamestown was rescued from the brink of failure. Although it was close to being deserted, Jamestown persevered and is now known as the oldest continuous settlement by the English.

John Smith's Impact on Jamestown

It had only been eight months since John Smith left Jamestown, but it was barely recognizable. The fort was in ruins, almost 90% of the colonists had died, and those left were starving and desperate to return to England. When John was in charge, he had the respect of the American Indians, and he motivated the colonists to work together so everyone would survive and Jamestown would prosper. If John Smith had remained in Jamestown, there may not have been a "starving time." He was resourceful and would have figured out a way to provide food for all. But without John Smith, Jamestown was not able to continue successfully and was nearly abandoned. John Smith was essential to the success of Jamestown becoming the first permanent English settlement in America.

John Smith Tries Again...and Again...and Again to Return to America

John Smith returned to England, and with proper medical treatment, recovered from his injuries. He was surprised to find himself a published author. While in Virginia, he had written a letter to a friend describing his experiences in Virginia. When the friend in England received the letter, he had it published as a book. By publishing John's letter, the friend made John Smith the first American author in English.

The book was titled, *A True Relation of Such Occurances and Accidents of Noate as Hath Happened in Virginia since the Planting of that Company.* (That's quite a title; don't you think?)

John spent the next several years writing books about his experiences in Virginia. He was obsessed with America and wanted nothing more than to return to the rugged land that had captured his heart. Unfortunately, the Virginia Company refused to send him back because they didn't like his brash manner and tough tactics.

In 1614, John was hired to go on a fishing trip off the coast of what is now known as Massachusetts and Maine. As he gazed out at the shore, he saw fertile land and friendly American Indians. He thought this would be an excellent location to start a colony, so he made a detailed map of the coastline. He called the area "New England," the name we still use today. Modern day historians believe John Smith's exploration of the New England area and detailed map were incredibly valuable. This alone would have made him famous and forever in our history books.

John decided he didn't need the Virginia Company to sponsor his return trip to America. He would organize his own expedition. He worked hard gathering supporters, crew, money, and colonists.

Finally in 1615, John had everything he needed. He was excited to be on his way back to America. It was a beautiful spring day when his ship set sail... and fell apart almost immediately. They turned around and barely made it back to the harbor safely before the ship took on too much water and sank.

John was determined. He set to work right away to secure another ship for the voyage. By June he was once again ready to set sail. John breathed a sigh of relief as the ship safely left the harbor. Unfortunately, his luck would not last. Before long, they had unwanted visitors – pirates were on the horizon! After a chase that lasted for two days, the pirate ship finally caught up with John's ship. John was afraid the pirates would destroy his ship, so he allowed them on board to talk. Imagine John's surprise when he realized he knew the pirates! He served in the military with some of them. They invited John to join them, but he said no thanks. They allowed him to sail on. He talked his way out of another conflict!

John again breathed a sigh of relief, but it didn't last long. Soon more pirates were chasing them. This time it was two French pirate ships. The pirates fired their cannon at John's ship. Frustrated and desperate, John yelled at the pirates, telling them he would burn his own ship and all of its contents before he would let them have it! They believed this crazy Englishman and quickly sailed away. John ordered his frazzled crew to sail on.

The very next day, four French pirate ships surrounded John's ship. Captain Smith went on board one pirate ship to try to talk his way out of this perilous situation, but his crew had other ideas. They had had enough of these dangerous, pirate-infested waters. Once the pirates were distracted talking with Captain Smith, his men set sail and escaped, leaving their Captain with the pirates!

The pirates held John captive for several weeks. He escaped in a small boat during a thunderous storm. The howling winds and massive waves sunk the pirate ship, but John stayed alive in his small boat. He baled water as quickly as he could to prevent the tiny boat from sinking. He made his way to a small island half dead, cold, and hungry. Some hunters found John and helped him to safety. John had written a 60-page book while he was held captive on board the pirate ship. He had it published in 1616 when he returned to England. It was quite possibly the only book ever written onboard a pirate ship. It was called, *A Description of New England*.

This was the last attempt John would make to reach America. Instead, he spent the rest of his days writing books, telling stories of his glory days to anyone who would listen, and spending time visiting friends.

John left Virginia in 1609 but spent the next 22 years writing about it and trying to go back. He could not stop thinking about this land for the rest of his life. It's sad that he never made it back to fulfill his dream, but that didn't stop him from writing several books encouraging others to go to America.

John Smith's Final Days

John Smith published his last book, *Advertisements for the Unexperienced Planters of New England, or Anywhere* in

1631 shortly before he died. Up until the end, he wrote about the land he grew to love. He would undoubtedly be pleased that America has fulfilled his vision as a place where hard work and perseverance can lead to success for any person regardless of social status.

John Smith died quietly in his bed on June 21, 1631, at the age of 51. It is not known what he died of, but he was very weak in his final days and barely able to write.

It seems odd that the soldier who escaped death so many times before ended up surrendering his life quietly to sickness. While history remembers John for his role with the Powhatan Indians and Pocahontas, you have learned that there was much more to John Smith. He was a farm boy who grew to be a man who lived a life full of adventure. He conquered enemies, survived storms, suffered injuries, endured slavery, outwitted pirates, defeated rivals, negotiated with American Indians, and played a vital role in the success of Jamestown.

Remembering Captain John Smith

John Smith was an underdog. He was a farmer's son who was never expected to be remembered throughout history. But even when the odds were stacked against him and there seemed to be no hope left, John's bravery and determination allowed him to remain steadfast.

John Smith wasn't wealthy or charming, but he was exactly what America needed. He had a unique blend of determination, common sense, and an ability to communicate with all types of people. These qualities enabled him to help Jamestown survive and become the first permanent English settlement in America. Because of John Smith, Jamestown became birthplace of the United States - Land of the Free, Home of the Brave.

John saw America's unlimited potential. Where others looked to America as a way to become rich quickly, he saw its promise. He saw a place where *any* man could make a life for himself through hard work and determination, not because he was born into the right family. And that is just what America became – a place where every person determines his or her own future – where the American Dream is a reality. John Smith was a true visionary and the American ideal.

53250676R00039

Made in the USA
San Bernardino, CA
10 September 2017